MW00604337

U.S. HISTORY BITES

Written by Solomon Schmidt

This is dedicated to my parents, who have
taught me so much about faith and life,
inspired me, and helped me with this book.

To my Great Grandpa Wilfred Aderman, who
is an inspiration to me for his strong faith,
hard work, and dedication to his family
and country. I admire him greatly for his role
in American history.

To Pastor Kevin and Mrs. Backus for
being so kind, loving, and encouraging to
me and my family.

I love you all and thank God for you.

A Note From the Author

U.S. History Bites includes thirty topics from American history that I think everyone should know. To enhance comprehension, it also includes vocabulary and review questions for each section, along with a glossary.

Parents, this book serves as a great read-aloud, but can also be enjoyed by independent readers in the earlier grades. It can be used as the main text for any American history curriculum or as a supplement alongside others. It is the perfect tool to help introduce children (and adults) to foundational United States history.

I really hope you enjoy it.

TABLE OF CONTENTS

☆☆☆☆☆☆☆☆☆☆☆☆☆☆☆

1 Christopher Columbus and Exploration (1400s)

Christopher Columbus

Several hundred years ago, people did not know America existed. It was not until an Italian explorer named Christopher Columbus came along that people learned there was a whole other world out there.

Christopher Columbus was born in Italy in 1451. When he was young, he always dreamed about going to sea and exploring.

When Columbus grew up, he wanted to find a faster way to get to a place called India. So he decided to head west to find a different route.

There was a problem, though. Columbus needed

money to buy ships and food for the trip. He asked many kings and queens for money, but they all said no. Finally, Queen Isabella of Spain decided to buy Columbus three ships named the *Santa Maria, Nina,* and *Pinta.* In just a short time, Columbus not only had three ships, but also enough food and water to make the trip to India.

The journey took a very long time, but in 1492 Columbus finally landed his ships on a group of **islands** called the Bahamas, very close to America. The problem was, he thought he had landed in India, and because of this, he named the people there "Indians."

Columbus became famous for his trip across the Atlantic Ocean. Even though Columbus did not discover America, he inspired other men to explore. Some of those men eventually settled in America and began **colonies** there.

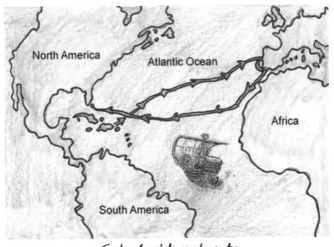

Columbus' travel route

REVIEW BITES

VOCABULARY

<u>Islands</u> – Small pieces of land that are completely surrounded by water

<u>Colonies</u> – Lands that are ruled by a far away country

FUN FACT

America was named after a Spanish merchant named Amerigo Vespucci. He traveled to America seven years after Columbus' first voyage.

REVIEW QUESTIONS

1. Who paid for three ships so that Christopher Columbus could go to India?

2. What did Columbus discover in 1492?

3. Did Columbus discover America?

The Pilgrims (Early 1600s)

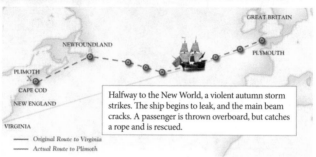

Halfway to the New World, a violent autumn storm strikes. The ship begins to leak, and the main beam cracks. A passenger is thrown overboard, but catches a rope and is rescued.

Mayflower travel route

In the early 1600s, there was a group of people in England who did not want the King of England telling them how to worship God. They were very brave and **devout** Christians. Christians are people who believe in Jesus Christ as their Lord and Savior and follow the teachings of the Bible.

The King of England would not allow certain Christians to practice their own **religion** and he wanted them to follow his rules. If they did not obey the King's rules, he would persecute them. So one group of Christians decided to separate from the Church of England and leave the country. They are known as the Separatists.

The Separatists left England and sailed to a new home in Holland, where they could worship God freely. They lived in Holland for about ten years, but eventually, they had problems there, too, and decided to leave.

The Separatists heard about America and thought it would be a good place to live and worship God freely. So in 1620, they set out on a long journey (called a pilgrimage) to America. This is why the Separatists are referred to as the Pilgrims (because they made a pilgrimage to America).

The Pilgrims sailed across the Atlantic Ocean on a ship called the *Mayflower*. The voyage was extremely long and difficult and many of the Pilgrims became very ill. After almost two months at sea, the Pilgrims finally made it to the New World. In 1620, they landed in Plymouth, Massachusetts and established the Plymouth Colony.

After they arrived in Plymouth, the Pilgrims eventually met a new people group. The Native Americans, also known as the Indians, helped the Pilgrims survive by teaching them how to plant corn and other types of food.

Eventually, all their hard work and suffering turned to blessings. The Pilgrims were so grateful for their bountiful harvest that they decided to celebrate with the Indians by having a large feast to thank God for all He had done for them. (A feast is when people get together to eat a lot of food and celebrate a special event.) We now celebrate a feast each year in America on Thanksgiving Day. We do this in honor of all that God had done for the Pilgrims and all that He has done for us.

REVIEW BITES

VOCABULARY

Devout - Caring a lot about a religion

Religion - When people believe in God or gods

Pilgrims - People who take long journeys for religious reasons

FUN FACT

In America, there was an Indian named Squanto, who helped the Pilgrims learn how to grow food.

REVIEW QUESTIONS

1. Why did the Separatists leave England?

2. Where did the Separatists go after they left England?

3. Where did the Separatists sail to after Holland?

3 The First Great Awakening (1734-1750)

A preacher teaching people about the Bible

During the First Great Awakening, **preachers** taught people about the Bible and how to live a holy life. The preachers taught in a very powerful way. They helped people realize the wrong things (sins) they were doing and helped them understand how to start behaving better based on the Bible. Because of this, many people repented of their sins and became Christians. Christians are people who believe in Jesus Christ as their Lord and Savior and follow the teachings of the Bible.

Jonathan Edwards was a very popular preacher during this time. His published works were widely read in America and England and helped fuel the Great Awakening.

Across the sea in Europe, two brothers, John and Charles Wesley, also became preachers. They traveled around England and many other places telling people about Jesus Christ. People who follow the Wesleys' teachings are called Wesleyans or Methodists.

Another man named George Whitefield met the Wesley brothers while in England. He followed some of John and Charles Wesley's teachings, but not all. Whitefield was a Calvinist, but the Wesley brothers were Arminians.

Like the Wesley brothers, George Whitefield also became a famous preacher during this time and led many people to become Christians all over Europe and America. He once preached to a large crowd in Philadelphia, Pennsylvania. Benjamin Franklin was in the crowd and was very impressed with Whitefield's speaking abilities. Eventually, the two men became very close friends.

Jonathan Edwards

REVIEW BITES

VOCABULARY

<u>Preacher</u> – A man who teaches the truth about the Bible and Jesus Christ during a sermon in church

FUN FACT

Jonathan Edwards wrote a well-known sermon called "Sinners in the Hands of an Angry God" and a famous treatise called *Freedom of the Will.*

REVIEW QUESTIONS

1. When was the First Great Awakening?

2. Name one famous preacher from the First Great Awakening.

3. What are people called who follow John Wesley's teachings?

1. 1734-1750 2. Jonathan Edwards, John Wesley, Charles Wesley, or George Whitefield 3. Wesleyans or Methodists

4 The French and Indian War (1756-1763)

George Washington during the French and Indian War

One hundred years after the Pilgrims came to America, many of the settlers from England and France started moving inland. Each of these two countries wanted to own a lot of land in America.

England owned much of the Eastern United States and France wanted it. France controlled an area called Canada and England wanted that.

The lands that England owned were called colonies. The colonists (people who lived in the colonies) helped the English take away land from the French, and the Indians tried to help the French take away land from the English.

One English colonist named George Washington was sent to capture a **fort** and take it away from the French and their Indian **allies**. He had a battle with the French that started the war between England and France. This war was called the French and Indian War because the French and Indians fought together against England and her colonies.

The English and French fought many battles. In one battle, the English won the entire country of Canada. Eventually, the French and the Indians knew that the English would win the war, so they signed a **treaty** with the English to end the fighting. This meant that England had won the French and Indian War.

Different territories during the war

REVIEW BITES

VOCABULARY

Fort – A place where soldiers live and defend against other soldiers who are trying to attack them

Allies – Countries or people that fight on the same side together

Treaty – An agreement between countries

FUN FACT

The French and Indian War was also called the Seven Years War because it lasted seven years.

REVIEW QUESTIONS

1. Who fought with the French as their allies?

2. Who had a battle with the French and the Indians that started the French and Indian War?

3. Who won the French and Indian War?

5 The Boston Tea Party (1773)

The Patriots throwing tea into the Boston Harbor

After England won the French and Indian War, the English government had no money because they had spent all of it during the war. In order to get money, King George III of England made the colonists in America pay a lot of **taxes**. This made some Americans very angry including one group of people called the Patriots. The Patriots did not like the English government and its taxes.

One thing the colonists had to pay high taxes on was tea. This made the Patriots especially angry because many colonists drank tea every day.

In 1773, the English government sent three ships loaded with tea to Boston, Massachusetts. They were going to tax the colonists for all the tea on the ships. Because of this, the Patriots in Boston made a plan to rebel against the English government. They planned to climb aboard the three ships and throw all the tea into the water of the Boston Harbor. They did not want there to be any more taxes on tea.

So on the night of December 16, 1773, the Patriots dressed up as Indians so people would not recognize them. Then, they went onto the three English ships and dumped all the tea into the water. This is known as the Boston Tea Party and it caused big problems between the Patriots and the English government.

Boston, Massachusetts

REVIEW BITES

VOCABULARY

<u>Taxes</u> - Money that people have to pay to the government

FUN FACT

Some of the Patriots who helped with the Boston Tea Party were Samuel Adams, Joseph Warren, and Paul Revere.

REVIEW QUESTIONS

1. What were the Patriots angry about?

2. When was the Boston Tea Party?

3. What did the Patriots do the night of the Boston Tea Party?

1. Taxes, mainly the tax on tea 2. December 16, 1773 3. Dressed up as Indians and dumped all the tea that was on the English ships into the Boston Harbor

6 The American Revolution (1775-1783)

George Washington crossing the icy Delaware River

After the Boston Tea Party, the English government kept doing things to anger the American colonists. So the Americans decided that they wanted to form their own country, apart from England. To become their own country, the colonists started a war in 1775 against the English called the American **Revolution**. It is also sometimes referred to as the Revolutionary War or the War for Independence.

During this time, an American named Thomas Jefferson wrote a very important document called the Declaration of Independence. This document told King George III of England that America wanted to be independent or separate from England.

The Americans chose George Washington to lead

their army during the American Revolution. He led the army through many battles, such as the Battle at Princeton and the Battle at Trenton.

The English army was very powerful and well organized. The American army did not know a lot about fighting and it seemed like the English would win. Even though the Americans won important battles like the Battle at Trenton, many of them still worried that the English would beat their small army.

To solve this problem, the Americans asked the French to help them fight. The French eventually agreed to fight against England, and in 1781, the Americans and the French defeated the English at the Battle of Yorktown. A treaty was later signed in 1783, which officially ended the fighting.

The Americans had won the War for Independence and now had their own country. However, they still had many problems to work out.

George Washington praying at Valley Forge

REVIEW BITES

VOCABULARY

Revolution – 1. A war against a government

2. A time when things change

FUN FACT

One of the French soldiers who came to America was Marquis de Lafayette. He and George Washington became good friends.

REVIEW QUESTIONS

1. Who wrote the Declaration of Independence?

2. Who led the American army during the
War for Independence?

3. What battle did the French
and Americans win against the English?

1. Thomas Jefferson 2. George Washington
3. The Battle of Yorktown

The United States Constitution

President George Washington

After gaining independence from England, the Americans needed to set up their own **government**. The leaders at that time, called the Continental Congress, divided America into thirteen **states**. The thirteen states that had once belonged to England each wanted their own government. Bigger states like Virginia wanted more people from their state to be in the government. Smaller states like Maryland did not think that was fair.

In order to try and resolve the differences between the states, the members of the Continental Congress wrote a document called the **Constitution**. The U.S.

Constitution described what American government would be like. It also explained the responsibilities of the American president and the responsibilities of the people who would represent the citizens of each state (called representatives). Bigger states would have more representatives than the smaller states.

On September 17, 1787, the Continental Congress signed the U.S. Constitution. This made the Constitution the official document of the American government.

Later, on April 30, 1789, under the Constitution, George Washington was unanimously elected to become America's first president.

Although the Constitution was very helpful, many Americans were unhappy that it did not give them certain rights or freedoms to do the things they wanted to do. So the Continental Congress wrote another document called the Bill of Rights. This gave Americans certain rights and freedoms and also limited the government's power over the people.

The Constitution and the Bill of Rights are very important parts of American government. They are so important that other countries have been inspired by them and created their own similar documents.

VOCABULARY

<u>Government</u> – A system that rules a country

<u>States</u> – Separate pieces of land that make up a country

<u>Constitution</u> – A document that explains a country's laws

FUN FACT

James Madison is known as the father of the Constitution because he contributed the most to the document.

REVIEW QUESTIONS

1. What was created to explain how the American government would work?

2. When did George Washington become the first United States president?

3. What was created to explain Americans' freedoms and rights?

1. The U.S. Constitution 2. In 1789 3. The Bill of Rights

A preacher talking to a lot of people

During the Second Great Awakening, **preachers** taught people about the Bible and how to live a holy life. The preachers taught large crowds of people in tents and sometimes stood on tree stumps, shouting their messages to the crowds. They taught in a very powerful way and helped people realize the wrong things (sins) they were doing. They also helped them understand how to start behaving better based on the Bible. As a result, many people repented of their sins and became Christians. Christians are people who believe in Jesus Christ as their Lord and Savior and follow the teachings of the Bible.

Preachers taught all over America during the Second Great Awakening. Some preachers even went out west to tell others about Jesus Christ.

One famous preacher during this time was Charles Finney. One thing Finney became popular for was the use of an "anxious bench" at the front of the congregation. People at his meetings would come to the bench to request prayer.

Charles Finney

REVIEW BITES

VOCABULARY

<u>Preacher</u> – A man who teaches the truth about the Bible and Jesus Christ during a sermon in church

FUN FACT

James McGready was one of the most important preachers of the Second Great Awakening in the American Frontier.

REVIEW QUESTIONS

1. What did preachers teach about during the Second Great Awakening?

2. Who was a famous preacher during the Second Great Awakening?

1. Jesus Christ and the Bible 2. Charles Finney

9 The Louisiana Purchase (1803-1806)

Lewis and Clark with Sacajawea

President Thomas Jefferson

In 1801, Thomas Jefferson became the 3rd President of the United States of America. At that time, the thirteen states only made up a small part of what America is today. There was a lot of land in America that had not been explored yet. President Jefferson wanted to make America bigger by adding states out West.

So President Jefferson bought a lot of land from France called the Louisiana **Territory**. This purchase of land is called the Louisiana **Purchase**.

President Jefferson decided to send two men named Meriwether Lewis and William Clark to explore the new land. Lewis and Clark took many men with them. They explored mountains and forests and met many Indians along the way. One Indian woman named Sacajawea helped Lewis and Clark explore the land.

Lewis and Clark discovered many things. After three years of exploration, they went back to President Jefferson and told him all about the things they had found. Many years later, several states were formed in the Louisiana Territory.

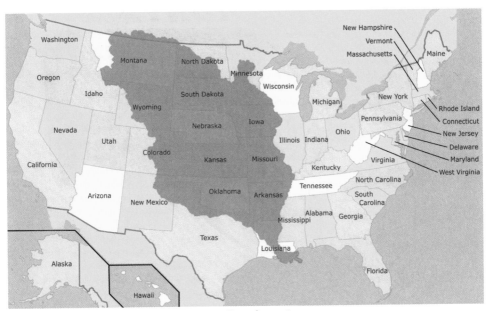

Louisiana Purchase in green

REVIEW BITES

VOCABULARY

<u>**Territory**</u> – A piece of land that is not a state

<u>**Purchase**</u> – Something that a person buys

FUN FACT

When Lewis and Clark came back to President Jefferson, they brought him a prairie dog as a present.

REVIEW QUESTIONS

1. What did President Jefferson buy from France?

2. What two men explored the Louisiana Territory?

3. Who helped Lewis and Clark explore the land?

1. The Louisiana Territory 2. Meriwether Lewis and William Clark 3. Sacajawea

Francis Scott Key

Original copy of the
Star Spangled Banner

From 1809-1817, James Madison was the president of America. During this time, England began doing bad things to Americans. In 1812, English sailors kidnapped American sailors and forced them to join the English Navy. This was very cruel, and it made many Americans angry. Because of this, President Madison declared war on England in 1812.

Between 1812 and 1814, the Americans won many battles at sea with their navy and also on land with their army. One time, the English Navy attacked Fort

McHenry in Baltimore, Maryland. English ships fired numerous cannonballs at the fort. The Battle at Fort McHenry lasted for many hours, but eventually, the Americans won.

A man named Francis Scott Key had witnessed the entire battle. He was so excited that the Americans had won that he wrote a famous poem about the battle called the *Defense of Fort McHenry.* Many years later, this poem was turned into the *Star Spangled Banner* and became America's national anthem. This song is still sung today at special events.

In 1814, England lost the war and America and England signed a treaty that officially ended the War of 1812.

President James Madison

REVIEW BITES

VOCABULARY

<u>Navy</u> – An entire force of ships that fight for a country

FUN FACT

James Madison was the smallest U.S. president. He was 5'4" tall and weighed less than 100 pounds.

REVIEW QUESTIONS

1. What made the Americans angry
at the English?

2. At what fort did Francis Scott Key
write a poem that later became known as
the *Star Spangled Banner?*

3. Who won the War of 1812?

David Crockett

David Crockett was born in Tennessee in 1786. His family called him Davy.

Davy loved to hunt all kinds of animals, but he especially loved to hunt bears. People even made up stories about him killing a bear when he was only three years old.

When Davy got older, he decided to help the Americans fight the Indians in Alabama. This is known as the Creek Indian War. Davy joined the fighting under General Andrew Jackson. He was a very smart and brave soldier.

Davy was also an adventurer and an explorer. He was so curious about the West that he decided to move his family there. Because Davy bravely explored and traveled to the West, he is Known as "The King of the Wild **Frontier**."

Davy loved being with his family, but he longed for more adventure. He heard that the people in the Texas **territory** were fighting against Mexico for their independence. Davy thought that sounded like an exciting adventure, so he left the West and went to help the Texans fight. He met up with a group of about 150 Texans at a fort called the Alamo.

One day during this fight, 5,000 Mexican soldiers came to capture the Alamo. Davy and the Texans Knew that they were outnumbered, but they did not give up.

Davy and the Texans fought the Mexicans for weeks and held out as long as they could, but eventually they were defeated. Davy Crockett died at the Alamo in 1836.

The Alamo in Texas

VOCABULARY

<u>**Frontier**</u> – A large area of land that has not been explored

<u>**Territory**</u> – A piece of land that is not a state

FUN FACT

At one time, David Crockett was so popular that many Americans thought he should run for U.S. President.

REVIEW QUESTIONS

1. In what state did Davy fight under General Andrew Jackson?

2. Where did Davy take his family?

3. Where did Davy die in 1836?

12 Immigration (1820-1930)

Ellis Island near New York City

In 1820, **immigration** began in America. Foreign people, called immigrants, came to America from countries such as Italy, Sweden, and Ireland. People traveled to America from all over the world.

Some immigrants came to America because they were very poor and hoped to get jobs and live a better life. Some immigrants came because they were not free to worship God in their own country.

Most immigrants sailed on boats all the way across the Atlantic Ocean to get to America. It was a very dangerous journey. The ships would take the immigrants to a place called Ellis Island, near New York City. Once they arrived, the immigrants were required to go through medical and legal inspections before they could enter America. When the inspectors were sure that the immigrants were ready to come into the country, they would make them American **citizens**.

Between 1820 and 1930, more than 37 million immigrants came to America. Each one of these immigrants had found a new life in America, the land of the free.

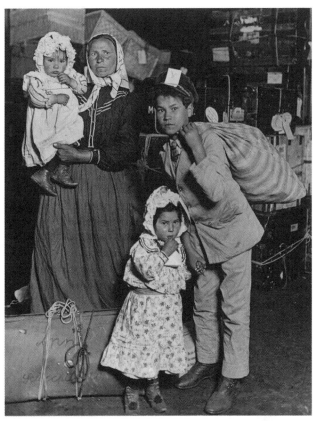

Immigrant family in the Baggage Room of Ellis Island

REVIEW BITES

VOCABULARY

Immigration - When people leave their country to live in another country

Citizens - People who are members of a country

FUN FACT

We now enjoy a wide variety of foods in America because of the many people who have come to live here from all over the world.

REVIEW QUESTIONS

1. From what countries did some immigrants come?

2. Where did immigrants go to be inspected?

3. How many immigrants came to America between 1820 and 1930?

1. Italy, Sweden, and Ireland 2. Ellis Island
3. More than 37 million

48

The Trail of Tears
(1838-1839)

The Cherokee Indians traveling out west

When immigrants came to America, more and more land was taken up in the East. At the time, Indians owned a large part of the land in America. People thought that if they moved the Indians to the West, there would be more open land for immigrants in the East.

Because of this, Congress passed the Indian Removal Act in 1830. This law said that the American government was allowed to take land from the Indians and make them live on land in the West.

There were five main Indian tribes involved in the

Removal Act: the Cherokee, Chickasaw, Choctaw, Creek, and Seminole tribes. The Chickasaw and Choctaw tribes agreed to leave and go out west, but while on their journey in 1831, many died from **starvation**. Because of this, the other three Indian tribes did not want to go west.

Eventually, the Seminole and Creek Indian tribes were forced by American soldiers to move west, but the Cherokee Indians tried for several years to keep their land in the East. American President Andrew Jackson told U.S. soldiers to force the Cherokee Indians to move west.

The Cherokee's long and hard journey took them a whole year, between 1838 and 1839. During this time, many of the Cherokee Indians died. Because of the Cherokee's suffering, their journey is called the Trail of Tears.

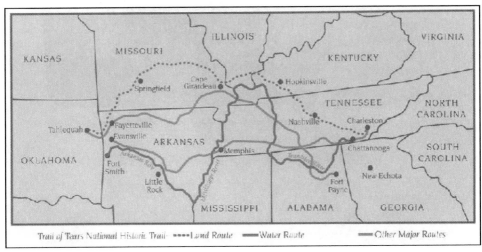

Indians moved from right to left on the Trail of Tears

REVIEW BITES

VOCABULARY

<u>Starvation</u> – When people do not have enough food to eat

FUN FACT

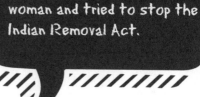

John Ross was an American man with Cherokee relatives. He was married to an Indian woman and tried to stop the Indian Removal Act.

REVIEW QUESTIONS

1. Which law allowed the American government to take the Indians' land and force them to move out west?

2. What two Indian tribes went out west first?

3. What is the journey of the Cherokee Indians called?

1. The Indian Removal Act 2. Chickasaw and Choctaw
3. The Trail of Tears

People traveling west in a covered wagon

Even though the Indian Removal Act opened up a lot of land in the East, more and more immigrants kept coming to America and taking up land. Because of this, some Americans thought about moving out west. Since cars had not been invented yet, people had to travel on horseback or in covered wagons.

Westward Expansion in America began when people took covered wagons out west to Oregon. The route they traveled on was called the Oregon Trail and it led them all the way across the country.

Many people started traveling on the Oregon Trail. It was a very long and difficult journey because of all the mountains and deserts along the way.

Some people also traveled to California, and in 1849, a group of **settlers** discovered gold there. This caused many other people to want to move to California in hopes of finding gold and becoming rich.

The people who went looking for gold were called "Forty-Niners." They were named this because the "gold rush" in California started in 1849.

Later, in 1869, workers built a transcontinental railroad in America. This meant that the railroad extended all the way across the country. This was a much faster way to travel than covered wagons and became a popular means of transportation.

The Oregon Trail

REVIEW BITES

VOCABULARY

<u>Settlers</u> - People who move to settle in a new area

FUN FACT

Another way to get to the West was to sail all the way down and around South America and then up to California. This was a very long journey, but was still faster than traveling on land.

REVIEW QUESTIONS

1. What did people originally travel in to go out west?

2. What was the name of the route that people traveled on to go out west?

3. What were the people called who looked for gold in California?

4. What was built across America in 1869?

15 The Civil War (1861-1865)

A battle during the Civil War

At the time of the founding fathers, **slavery** was legal and practiced in all thirteen colonies. Slavery was when black people were owned by white people and were forced to work for them.

During the 1780s, some of the northern states ended slavery, which is why they were called free states. By 1804, all of the northern states had made slavery illegal. However, slavery was still legal in the southern states, which is why they were called slave states.

Some Americans in the North (called Northerners) were not bothered by slavery and just thought it should stay in the South. While other Northerners thought that slavery was wrong and should be abolished everywhere. However, some of the people in the southern states (called Southerners) and some Northerners did not want the U.S. federal government telling the states what to do, no matter what the issue was.

So between 1860 and 1861, eleven southern states decided to separate from the United States and form their own new country called the Confederate States of America (Confederacy). When they did this, it was called seceding from the Union. The United States government thought it was wrong for the southern states to do this and was willing to fight to restore the Union. This was called The War Between the States, also known as the Civil War.

Confederate states in red

The North and South fought the first battle of the war in 1861. General Ulysses S. Grant led the Northern army and General Robert E. Lee led the Southern army.

Abraham Lincoln was the American president during this time. He wanted the states to be united again into one country. One of his famous quotes was, "A house divided against itself will not stand."

Finally, in the spring of 1865, after four long and difficult years of battles, the South lost the war and **surrendered** to the North. One of the many battles took place in Gettysburg, Pennsylvania. It was the bloodiest battle of them all and involved the largest number of casualties. It is estimated that over 750,000 people died during the Civil War.

Many Americans were angry with some of the decisions that President Lincoln made. In early 1865, a Southerner named John Wilkes Booth and a few other men planned to kidnap President Lincoln in exchange for the release of some Confederate soldiers. However, after hearing the president give a speech about wanting to give black people voting rights, John Wilkes Booth became very angry and decided to kill President Lincoln instead.

On April 14, 1865, while President Lincoln was

attending a play at the Ford's Theatre in Washington, D.C., Mr. Booth killed him. This happened just days after the official end of the war.

Later that same year, in December 1865, after President Lincoln had died, the American government changed the U.S. Constitution so that there could be no more slavery in America. This is known as the 13th Amendment and is what finally freed all slaves.

As an aside – During the War Between the States, some slaves in the South wanted to be free and escaped to the North on the Underground Railroad. This was not a real railroad. It was a secret way for slaves in the South to escape to the North. There were some people who secretly helped the slaves get to freedom. One of those people groups were the Quakers. They were very religious people who believed slavery was wrong.

General
Ulysses S. Grant

General
Robert E. Lee

President
Abraham Lincoln

REVIEW BITES

VOCABULARY

<u>Slavery</u> – When black people were owned by white people and were forced to work for them

<u>Surrendered</u> – Gave up in a war

FUN FACT

In 1861, the southern states formed the Confederate States of America, and they elected Jefferson Davis to be their president.

REVIEW QUESTIONS

1. What caused many battles between the North and the South?

2. Who led the Northern army? Who led the Southern army?

3. Who lost the Civil War and when?

1. Many things including slavery
2. Ulysses S. Grant, |Robert E. Lee 3. The South, in 1865

16 The Industrial Revolution (1790-1908)

The Wright Brothers flying their plane for the first time

The Industrial **Revolution** was a time when Americans built new things called **inventions**. Many of these inventions are still used all around the world today.

During the Industrial Revolution, many intelligent people created some very useful things. These inventions made life much easier for people and also provided thousands of factory jobs.

During the 1700s and 1800s people used to gather cotton in fields. Slaves used to go out into the fields and pick cotton by hand, but it was very hard work and took a long time. So in 1794, a man named Eli Whitney invented the cotton gin. It was a machine that picked cotton much faster than people could.

In 1876, a man named Alexander Graham Bell invented the telephone. A few years later, in 1879, Thomas Edison invented the lightbulb.

Then, in 1903, two brothers named Orville and Wilbur Wright invented the first airplane. It took them many years and several failed attempts, but eventually, all their hard work and dedication paid off. Later, in 1908, Henry Ford invented an automobile (car) called the Model T.

The Industrial Revolution was one of the most advanced times in all of history. People went from using hand tools and basic machines to large power machines in factories. This led to mass production of many goods.

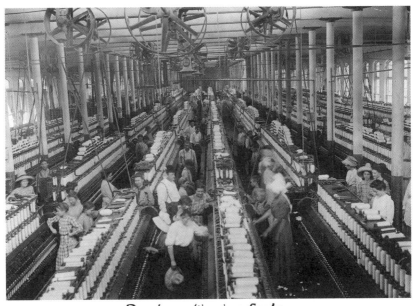

People working in a factory

REVIEW BITES

VOCABULARY

<u>Revolution</u> – 1. A war against a government
2. A time when things change

<u>Inventions</u> – Things that people create which have never been built before

FUN FACT

Before they started working on airplanes, the Wright Brothers owned a bicycle shop in Dayton, Ohio.

REVIEW QUESTIONS

1. Who invented the cotton gin?

2. When did Thomas Edison
   invent the lightbulb?

3. Who invented the Model T car?

1. Eli Whitney 2. 1879 3. Henry Ford

17 The Spanish-American War (1898)

Theodore Roosevelt and the Rough Riders

When Christopher Columbus sailed to the Bahamas, he had discovered a place called Cuba. It is a small **island** near the state of Florida. Since the King and Queen of Spain sent Columbus, and he discovered Cuba, it became a Spanish territory.

However, almost 400 years later, Cuba did not want to be ruled by Spain anymore. Just like America, Cuba wanted to become its own country.

At that time, William McKinley was the 25th President of America. He wanted to help Cuba break away from Spain. So he sent an American ship called the *Maine* to help the Cubans.

Sometime after the *Maine* had arrived in Cuba, it exploded in the water. This explosion killed thousands of sailors. Many Americans thought that the Spanish had blown up the ship. Because of the explosion, President McKinley declared war on Spain.

In April of 1898, the president sent many soldiers to Cuba to fight against Spain. One soldier named Theodore Roosevelt led a group of soldiers called the Rough Riders. Roosevelt and the Rough Riders fought against the Spanish on San Juan Hill in Cuba. It was a very long and difficult battle, but the Rough Riders eventually beat the Spanish.

In August of 1898, because of the Battle of San Juan Hill, Spain surrendered to the Americans. This ended the Spanish-American War.

Theodore Roosevelt went on to become the next American president after William McKinley.

President William McKinley

President Theodore Roosevelt

REVIEW BITES

VOCABULARY

<u>Island</u> – A small piece of land that is completely surrounded by water

FUN FACT

Theodore Roosevelt's men were called the Rough Riders because people thought they rode on horses. They actually didn't ride horses at all during the Battle of San Juan Hill, but they were very tough men.

REVIEW QUESTIONS

1. What happened in Cuba that made Americans angry and eventually started the Spanish-American War?

2. Who led the band of soldiers called the Rough Riders?

3. Which battle led to the end of the Spanish-American War?

1. A ship called the *Maine* exploded in Cuba and the Americans thought that the Spanish had done it 2. Theodore Roosevelt 3. The Battle of San Juan Hill

18

World War I (1914-1918)

Soldiers in trenches during a battle

Europe is a group of countries in another part of the world. Two countries in Europe named Germany and Austria-Hungary wanted to be very powerful. They wanted to take over other countries like England and France.

In 1914, a man from the country of Serbia **assassinated** Archduke Ferdinand, the leader of Austria-Hungary. Because of the assassination, Austria-Hungary attacked Serbia and this started a war called World War I. Italy and Germany joined together with Austria-Hungary to fight against England, France, and Russia.

At that time, Woodrow Wilson was the 28th President of America. He did not want America to enter the war in Europe.

But in 1915, the Germans sunk a ship called the *Lusitania*. There were many Americans on board who died. President Wilson was angry at the Germans, but he still did not want to join the war.

The countries in Europe kept fighting for two more years. By 1917, President Wilson finally decided to enter America into the war. America joined with England, France, and Russia. Surprisingly, Italy switched sides and fought against Germany too.

Because America's strong **military** was now involved, the war in Europe soon came to an end. In 1918, the Germans and the Austro-Hungarians surrendered.

Since so many countries around the world fought in this war, it is known as World War I.

Europe during World War I

President Woodrow Wilson

72

VOCABULARY

<u>Assassinated</u> – Murdered

<u>Military</u> – The entire force of soldiers, sailors, and pilots who protect a country

FUN FACT

One time during World War I, Germany sent a message to Mexico asking them to attack the United States, but Mexico never did. This message is known as the Zimmerman Telegram.

REVIEW QUESTIONS

1. Whose assassination led to World War I?

2. Which countries fought against Germany and Austria-Hungary?

3. What made President Wilson angry at the Germans?

19

The Great Depression (1929-1939)

A mother and her children during the Great Depression

In 1929, a bad time known as the Great **Depression** began. It was a very difficult time for many Americans. Many businesses failed and people lost their jobs. People had a hard time finding work and as a result, they became extremely poor.

To help the poor people who had lost their jobs, soup kitchens were opened. These were places where people could get free food. The soup kitchens helped many Americans survive through the Great Depression.

In 1933, Franklin D. Roosevelt (FDR) became America's 32nd president. He saw the desperate need of Americans during the Great Depression.

To try to help, President Roosevelt set up government programs that would provide jobs for people. Some programs were also created to help educate children because their parents could not afford to send them to school. These government programs were part of what was called the New Deal. Unfortunately, not all of these programs were beneficial for America.

It took ten years for the Great Depression to end. It wasn't until the early 1940s that the American economy finally started to recover because of wartime production. Slowly, businesses began doing better and people started finding jobs again.

People waiting outside a soup kitchen for food

President Franklin D. Roosevelt

REVIEW BITES

VOCABULARY

<u>Depression</u> – A time when businesses stop running and many people lose their jobs

FUN FACT

In 1929, Herbert Hoover was the 31st American president. Many Americans thought he was not doing a good job helping them during the Great Depression. Because of this, Americans elected Franklin D. Roosevelt to be the next president.

REVIEW QUESTIONS

1. What two main things started the Great Depression?

2. Who created government programs to try and help Americans during the Depression?

3. How long did the Great Depression last?

1. Businesses failed and many people lost their jobs 2. President Franklin D. Roosevelt 3. Ten years

20

World War II (1939-1945)

British Prime Minister
Winston Churchill

German leader Adolf Hitler

In the 1930s, Germany was still very angry that they had lost World War I. Adolf Hitler became the German leader in the early 1930s. He wanted **revenge** on countries like England because of World War I. So he started to build up an army of German soldiers known as the Nazis.

Hitler was a very wicked ruler who did cruel and evil things to people called the Jews. He is responsible for the death of over six million Jewish men, women, and children. This is known as the Holocaust.

The leader of England, named Winston Churchill,

saw that Hitler's power was growing and that another war was likely to start. Most people ignored Churchill, though, and did not think that there would be another world war.

Those people were wrong. On September 1, 1939, Hitler and his Nazis attacked the country of Poland. This started World War II.

During this time, Italy had a new leader named Benito Mussolini, and Japan had a new leader named Hirohito. Both of these men wanted to have a lot of power, so they joined forces with Hitler and began fighting against the other European countries. England, France, and many other countries fought against the Germans, Italians, and the Japanese.

Franklin D. Roosevelt (FDR) was the American President during World War II. Just like President Woodrow Wilson during World War I, he did not want America to enter the war.

Japanese leaders knew how powerful America was, and they looked for a way to weaken America. Japanese military leaders knew that a lot of America's Navy ships were located at Pearl Harbor in Hawaii. So the Japanese decided to attack there. The Americans had no idea that they were about to be ambushed.

In December of 1941, Japanese soldiers, led by Mitsuo Fuchida, secretly flew planes toward Pearl Harbor. On the morning of December 7th, 1941, the Japanese attacked Pearl Harbor in Hawaii. They bombed and destroyed many ships that were in America's Navy, including one called the *Arizona*. It was damaged more than any other ship. Sadly, over 2,000 American soldiers died at Pearl Harbor.

The Japanese also destroyed many planes that were in America's **Air Force**. Because of Pearl Harbor, President Roosevelt finally decided to enter America into World War II.

On June 6, 1944 the Allies (the countries fighting against Hitler) attacked the Nazis on the beaches of Normandy in France. This helped to free many European countries from Germany's power over them. June 6th is a very important day in the history of World War II and is known as D-Day.

World War II lasted for six years until the Axis (Germany and its allies) surrendered in 1945. Sadly, over 400,000 American soldiers died during this war. There is a World War II memorial for them in Washington, D.C.

Europe during World War II

My Great Grandpa Wilfred Aderman

Personal Note: My Great Grandpa Wilfred Aderman was in the U.S. Army at Pearl Harbor on December 7, 1941. He was getting his ammunition checked when all of a sudden, he was called outside to help defend the base at Pearl Harbor against the Japanese.

At age 94, he currently resides in Florida with my great grandma. I thank God for his bravery and willingness to serve our country and defend the freedoms we still enjoy today.

VOCABULARY

<u>Revenge</u> – To get back at someone because of something they did

<u>Air Force</u> – The part of a military in which pilots fight in planes

FUN FACT

One of the most famous American generals during World War II was Dwight D. Eisenhower. He went on to become the 34th United States President in 1953.

REVIEW QUESTIONS

1. What German leader began World War II?

2. Where did the Japanese attack the American Navy in 1941?

3. What major operation in 1944 helped to end World War II?

4. Who won World War II in 1945?

21 The Cold War (1945-1991)

President Harry Truman

Soviet leader Josef Stalin

Unlike most wars in history, no battles were fought during the Cold War. In this "war," countries used **threats** to scare each other. Even though no fighting ever occurred, people were still afraid of other countries.

The Cold War began after World War II. Russia (also known as the Soviet Union) and America each wanted different things to happen in Europe after World War II.

The Soviet Union leader, Josef Stalin, wanted European countries to become **communist** nations. This meant that the Soviet government would take away the Soviet people's rights and freedoms and control the way

85

they lived. Stalin was a very wicked ruler and did horrible things to the Soviet people.

At the beginning of the Cold War, Harry Truman was America's 33rd president. He wanted countries in Europe to become democratic. This meant that the government would give people their rights and freedoms. Eventually, many countries in Western Europe became democratic nations while other countries in Eastern Europe became communist nations.

During the Cold War, the Americans and Soviets were involved in many **conflicts** with each other including the Cuban Missile Crisis, the Berlin Wall, and the Space Race. In 1991, the Soviet Union's government finally fell apart, and this ended the Cold War after 46 years.

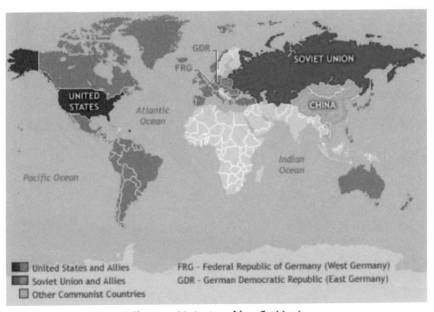

The world during the Cold War

REVIEW BITES

VOCABULARY

<u>Threats</u> - Things people say or do to scare others

<u>Communist</u> - A type of government that controls a society and takes away the private rights of its citizens

<u>Conflicts</u> - Arguments or wars between people

FUN FACT

The Cold War might sound like a strange name for a war. However, the word "cold" also means unfriendly. During the Cold War, the Soviet Union and America were unfriendly to each other.

REVIEW QUESTIONS

1. Instead of fighting battles, what did countries do during the Cold War?

2. What types of government did Eastern and Western Europe have?

3. When did the Soviet Union's government collapse, ending the Cold War?

4. How long did the Cold War last?

22 The Korean War (1950-1953)

Korean children standing in front of a tank

Many countries make up an area in the world called Asia. One of these countries is Korea.

At the end of World War II, America, England, and the Soviet Union were deciding what to do with Korea because during the war, the northern and southern parts of Korea had disagreed on many things. The foreign leaders decided to help lead Korea until the Koreans could rule themselves again. They divided Korea into two separate countries: North Korea and South Korea. They separated the country so both sides could solve their problems and become one country again later.

However, the problems were not fixed because North Korea became **communist** and South Korea became democratic. So with the help of the Soviet Union, North Korea attacked South Korea in 1950. This started the Korean War.

An American general named Douglas MacArthur took American soldiers to help South Korea. Three years later, in 1953, both North and South Korea agreed to a **ceasefire**. This ended the Korean War.

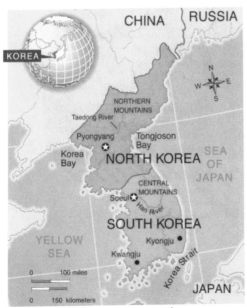

North and South Korea

General Douglas MacArthur

REVIEW BITES

VOCABULARY

Communist – A type of government that controls a society and takes away the private rights of its citizens

Ceasefire – An agreement that ends fighting in a war, but nobody wins

FUN FACT

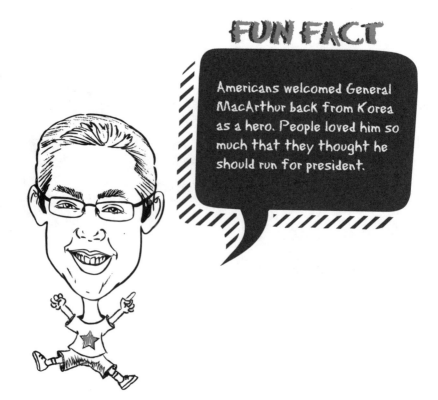

Americans welcomed General MacArthur back from Korea as a hero. People loved him so much that they thought he should run for president.

REVIEW QUESTIONS

1. Why did America, England, and the Soviet Union divide Korea into two countries?

2. What country helped communist North Korea invade South Korea in 1950?

3. When did both sides agree to a ceasefire?

1. So the countries could solve their problems and become one country again later 2. The Soviet Union 3. In 1953

Television (1926-Present)

A little girl watching an old television set

Television (TV) has been a large part of American culture for the past one hundred years. Most Americans watch several hours of television every day on something called the television set. An American named Philo Farnsworth invented the first television set in 1927.

For many years, people could only watch television in black and white. But, in 1954, color television was invented.

Some of the first and most popular TV shows in American History were **comedies**. Two of the most popular comedy shows were *I Love Lucy* and *Leave it to Beaver*.

I Love Lucy began in 1951. It was about a woman named Lucy and her husband, Ricky. In the show, they have many silly adventures with their friends, the Mertzes. This show ended in 1960.

Leave it to Beaver began in 1957. It was about a boy named Theodore, but everyone called him Beaver. In the show, Beaver has many adventures with his brother, Wally, and his parents. This show ended in 1963.

Television is still a big part of many people's lives today. Once considered a great **luxury**, many American homes now have multiple TV sets.

Advertisement for I Love Lucy

REVIEW BITES

VOCABULARY

<u>Comedies</u> - TV shows that are designed to make people laugh

<u>Luxury</u> - A costly comfort or privilege

FUN FACT

Another popular TV show in the 1950s was called, *Mister Ed*. Mister Ed was a talking horse. He and his owner, Wilbur, got into a lot of trouble on the show.

REVIEW QUESTIONS

1. When was color TV invented?

2. In the show, *I Love Lucy*, who are Ricky and Lucy's friends?

3. In the show, *Leave it to Beaver*, who is Theodore's brother?

1. In 1954 2. The Mertzes 3. Wally

Martin Luther King Jr. in Washington, D.C.

Even though slavery was not allowed in America anymore, some white people still thought that they were better than black people. Black people were **segregated**, which means they were separated from white people. Black people were not allowed to sit in the same bus seats as white people. They were also not allowed to drink at the same water fountains or attend the same schools as white people.

A black man named Martin Luther King Jr. (Junior) was sad about what was happening to black people in America. So in 1950, he started the Civil Rights Movement. This movement was made up of many black people who were working hard to give black people the same freedoms as white people.

Many people followed Martin Luther King Jr. and began to **protest** peacefully. One time, thousands of people went to Washington, D.C. to hear Dr. King give an inspirational speech called the *I Have a Dream* speech.

Because of the Civil Rights Movement, the U.S. government made a law in 1964 called the Civil Rights Act. This gave black people many freedoms. This was a great victory for Martin Luther King Jr. and his followers, but not every American was happy about the new changes.

In 1968, an angry white man named James Earl Ray **assassinated** Martin Luther King Jr. This made many Americans very sad and it divided the country. Thankfully though, because of Dr. King's hard work, black people have equal rights all throughout America today.

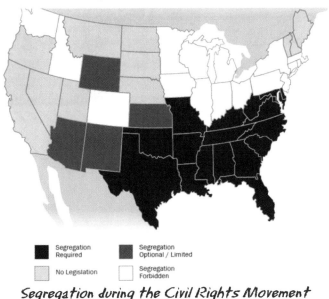

Segregation Required

Segregation Optional / Limited

No Legislation

Segregation Forbidden

Segregation during the Civil Rights Movement

REVIEW BITES

VOCABULARY

Segregated – Separated

Protest – To speak out against something

Assassinated – Murdered

FUN FACT

Rosa Parks was a black woman who refused to sit in the back of a bus. She was arrested for it, and this led to the Alabama Bus Boycott. As a result, the law was changed and black people were allowed to sit in the same seats as white people.

REVIEW QUESTIONS

1. What does segregation mean?

2. When did the Civil Rights movement begin and who led it?

3. What was the name of Martin Luther King Jr.'s famous speech?

The Space Race (1957-1969)

NASA's Kennedy Space Center in Florida

During the Cold War, the Americans and Soviets (another name for the Russians) began something called the Space Race. It is called a race because each country wanted to see who could do important things in outer space first.

The Soviets started the race in 1957, when they sent the first **satellite** into space. Immediately, Americans began the National Aeronautics Space Administration (NASA). NASA would help send Americans into space. However, the Russians won a part of the race when a Soviet named Yuri Gagarin became the first person to go into space. It seemed like the Soviets would win the Space Race, but America was about to do something extraordinary.

On July 20, 1969, an American **astronaut** named Neil Armstrong became the first person to walk on the moon! The Soviets knew that they could not do anything greater than this, and because of it, in 1969, they lost the Space Race.

Neil Armstrong on the moon

REVIEW BITES

VOCABULARY

Satellite – Something that is sent into space to get information about things

Astronaut – A scientist who goes into outer space

FUN FACT

Three American astronauts landed on the moon: Neil Armstrong, Buzz Aldrin, and Michael Collins. The reason Neil Armstrong is the most famous is because he stepped onto the moon first.

REVIEW QUESTIONS

1. Who was the first person to go into space?

2. Who was the first man to walk on the moon?

3. Who won the Space Race?

1. A Soviet named Yuri Gagarin
2. An American named Neil Armstrong 3. America

A missile that was sent to Cuba

Missiles are small rockets that can do a lot of damage. During the Cold War, America and the Soviet Union had a lot of powerful missiles. Many people were afraid that the countries would attack each other with them.

In 1962, John F. Kennedy was the 35th President of America. Fidel Castro was the leader of Cuba, and a man named Nikita Krushchev was the leader of the Soviet Union.

Krushchev and Castro were meeting in secret. They agreed that the Soviet Union would send missiles to Cuba to help protect them from attacks.

President Kennedy heard that there were missiles in Cuba. These missiles were located very close to America and could destroy a lot of land. People were afraid that Cuba would shoot the missiles at America.

President Kennedy and Soviet leader Krushchev met and talked with each other. Krushchev agreed to take the missiles out of Cuba. President Kennedy agreed not to attack Cuba unless Cuba attacked America. This conflict is known as the Cuban Missile Crisis.

Cuban leader Fidel Castro

President John F. Kennedy

REVIEW BITES

VOCABULARY

<u>Conflicts</u> - Arguments or wars between people

<u>Crisis</u> - A time of great trouble, danger, or difficulty

FUN FACT

During the Cuban Missile Crisis, some people told President Kennedy that he should attack Cuba. He did not listen because he did not want to start a war with Cuba.

REVIEW QUESTIONS

1. Who was the president of America during the Cuban Missile Crisis?

2. Who was the leader of Cuba during the Cuban Missile Crisis?

3. What did Soviet leader Krushchev send to Cuba?

1. John F. Kennedy 2. Fidel Castro 3. Missiles

27 The Vietnam War (1965-1975)

U.S. soldiers getting off a helicopter in Vietnam

There is a country in Asia called Vietnam. After World War II, Vietnam was separated into two countries: North Vietnam and South Vietnam.

North Vietnam became **communist** and South Vietnam was democratic. The people in North Vietnam wanted to **conquer** South Vietnam and attacked them in 1959.

America knew about the **tensions** going on in North and South Vietnam. So in 1964, President Lyndon B. Johnson sent a ship to Vietnam on a secret **mission**, but the North Vietnamese army destroyed the ship. Because of this, President Johnson sent American soldiers to fight in North Vietnam in 1965.

Over the next five years, more than 500,000 American soldiers fought in the Vietnam War. Some Americans did not agree with the war in Vietnam and they **protest**ed it. However, American soldiers continued to fight against North Vietnam.

In 1969, Richard Nixon became the 37th President of America and he started to pull American soldiers out of Vietnam. By 1973, all American soldiers were pulled out of Vietnam.

North Vietnam eventually conquered South Vietnam in 1975. They became one country again, but the communists ruled it. This finally ended the Vietnam War. Sadly, almost 60,000 American soldiers died in this war. There is a memorial for them in Washington, D.C., called the Vietnam War Memorial.

Vietnam War Memorial
in Washington, D.C.

President
Lyndon B. Johnson

REVIEW BITES

VOCABULARY

<u>Communist</u> – A type of government that controls a society and takes away the private rights of its citizens

<u>Conquer</u> – Defeat

<u>Tensions</u> – Problems

<u>Mission</u> – An important job

<u>Protest</u> – To speak out against something

FUN FACT

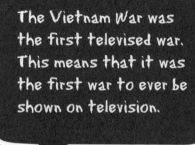

The Vietnam War was the first televised war. This means that it was the first war to ever be shown on television.

REVIEW QUESTIONS

1. What started the Vietnam War in 1965?

2. Which American President began to pull soldiers out of the Vietnam War?

3. Who won the Vietnam War in 1975?

Watergate Complex in Washington, D.C.

Political parties are groups of people that believe different things about how government should run. The two main political parties in America are the Republicans and the Democrats.

In 1969, a Republican named Richard Nixon became the 37th president of the United States. When he became president, he set up a group of people called the Plumbers.

In 1972, President Nixon told the Plumbers to break into a place called the Watergate Complex. This was a place where many important Democrats would meet.

The Plumbers hid small microphones in the building to record what the Democrats were saying. This would get President Nixon information about the Democrats and what they were planning to do.

Many Americans thought that it was very sneaky and dishonest for President Nixon to let the Plumbers break into the Watergate Complex. Sadly, President Nixon lied and said that he did not know about it. However, no matter what the president said, people did not believe him, and his problems kept getting worse.

Eventually, President Nixon knew he was going to be **impeached** because of his lies. So instead of having that happen, he **resigned** as president in 1974.

The reason this is important in American History is because President Nixon is the only president to have ever resigned from office.

President Richard Nixon

REVIEW BITES

VOCABULARY

Impeached – When a president loses his job because he did something very wrong

Resign – To give up something, like a job

FUN FACT

Plumbers are people who fix leaks in water pipes. President Nixon called his group of people the Plumbers because they were told to stop the leaking of secret government information to the media.

REVIEW QUESTIONS

1. What group did President Nixon set up to keep him out of trouble?

2. Where did the Plumbers break into in 1972?

3. Did President Nixon know about the plan to break into the Watergate Complex?

4. What did President Nixon do in 1974?

1. The Plumbers 2. The Watergate Complex
3. Yes 4. He resigned as president

The Berlin Wall (1989)

Two people in Germany looking over the Berlin Wall

During the Cold War (see section 21), the Berlin Wall was built to divide the country of Germany into two sections. One section was the West, and the other section was the East. West Germany had a free government, but East Germany had a **communist** government. The Berlin Wall was built to separate these two governments.

Many people, even families, were separated by the wall. For this reason, many Americans wanted the Berlin wall to be torn down.

In 1989, Ronald Reagan was the 40th President of America, and Mikhail Gorbachev was the leader of the Soviet Union (Russia). Even though the Soviet Union was communist, Gorbachev wanted to change things. President Reagan and Gorbachev worked together to end the Cold War.

Because of President Reagan and Gorbachev's work, the Berlin Wall was eventually torn down in 1989, and communism began to **decline** all over Europe.

President Reagan giving the Brandenburg Gate Address

President Ronald Reagan and
Soviet leader Mikhail Gorbachev

REVIEW BITES

VOCABULARY

Communist – A type of government that controls a society and takes away the private rights of its citizens

Decline – To decrease or become less

FUN FACT

In 1987, American President Ronald Reagan gave a very important speech. The most famous line from that speech was said to Soviet leader Mikhail Gorbachev. President Reagan said, "Mr. Gorbachev, tear down this wall!"

REVIEW QUESTIONS

1. Why was the Berlin Wall built?

2. Which two world leaders worked together to end the Cold War and tear down the Berlin Wall?

3. When was the Berlin Wall torn down?

1. To separate Western and Eastern Germany
2. American President Ronald Reagan and Soviet leader Mikhail Gorbachev 3. 1989

The World Trade Center before the 9/11 attack

A millennium is **1000** years. Another millennium began in the year 2000. People all over the world were very excited and celebrated it.

In 2001, George W. Bush became the 43rd President of America. He was the first U.S. President elected in the new millennium.

There is a place in the world called the Middle East. There are many countries that make up the Middle East and some of the people there hate America.

In September 2001, some **terrorists** from the Middle East decided to attack America with airplanes. There were two very tall buildings in New York City called the World Trade Center towers. On September 11, 2001, the terrorists crashed two planes into both towers. Over 2,000 people died. It was a very sad day in America.

Later that same day, more terrorists attacked another place called the Pentagon, which is near Washington D.C. Over 100 people died there.

Sadly, the terrorists were not done hurting Americans. More of them took over a third plane on that same day and were flying it to another place to attack. Some very brave people on that plane tried to stop the terrorists, but tragically, the plane crashed into a field in Pennsylvania and more people died. Many Americans were extremely sad and afraid.

President Bush gave a very important speech to try to help Americans feel better. He also decided to send soldiers to the Middle East to attack the terrorists. This started the Iraq War.

Remnants of the World Trade Center after 9/11

George W. Bush served eight years as President of the United States. Then in 2009, Barack Obama became the 44th President of the United States. This is very significant because he was the first black man to become an American president.

President George W. Bush

President Barack Obama's inauguration in 2009

REVIEW BITES

VOCABULARY

<u>**Terrorists**</u> – People who do things to hurt or scare other people

FUN FACT

In 2000, George W. Bush and Al Gore were both running for president. Bush won by a narrow margin, which means that he won by only a little bit.

REVIEW QUESTIONS

1. Where did terrorists attack on September 11, 2001?

2. Where else did terrorists attack on September 11, 2001?

3. Who was the first black man to be elected president?

Congratulations! You have finished reading *U.S. History Bites.*

I hope you have enjoyed it and will continue learning more about America's important history.

— Solomon

GLOSSARY

A

Air Force – The part of a military in which pilots fight in planes

Allies – Countries or people that fight on the same side together

Assassinated – Murdered

Astronaut – A scientist who goes into outer space

C

Ceasefire – An agreement that ends fighting in a war, but nobody wins

Citizens – People who are members of a country

Colonies – Lands that are ruled by a far away country

Comedies – TV shows that are designed to make people laugh

Communist – A type of government that controls a society and takes away the private rights of its citizens

Conflicts – Arguments or wars between people

Conquer – Defeat

Constitution – A document that explains a country's laws

Crisis – A time of great trouble, danger, or difficulty

D

Decline – To decrease or become less

Depression – A time when businesses stop running and many people lose their jobs

Devout – Caring a lot about a religion

Fort – A place where soldiers live and defend against other soldiers who are trying to attack them

Frontier – A large area of land that has not been explored

Government – A system that rules a country

Immigration – When people leave their country to live in another country

Impeached – When a president loses his job because he did something very wrong

Industrial – A word that describes when people make inventions

Inventions – Things that people create which have never been built before

Island – A small piece of land that is completely surrounded by water

Luxury – A costly comfort or privilege

Military – The entire force of soldiers, sailors, and pilots that protect a country

Mission – An important job

Navy – An entire force of ships that fight for a country

Pilgrims – People who take long journeys for religious reasons

Preacher – A man who teaches the truth about the Bible and Jesus Christ during a sermon in church

Protest – To speak out against something

Purchase – Something that a person buys

Religion – When people believe in God or gods

Resign – To give up something, like a job

Revenge – To get back at someone because of something they did

Revolution – 1. A war against a government
2. A time when things change

Satellite – Something that is sent into space to get information about things

Segregated – Separated

Settlers – People who move to settle in a new area

Slavery – When black people were owned by white people and were forced to work for them

Starvation – When people do not have enough food to eat

States – Separate pieces of land that make up a country

Surrendered – Gave up in a war

Taxes – Money that people have to pay to the government

Tensions – Problems

Territory – A piece of land that is not a state

Terrorists – People who do things to hurt or scare other people

Threats – Things people say or do to scare others

Treaty – An agreement between countries